THE QUANTOCKS

by Jillian Powell
with photographs by Julia Davey

Bossiney Books

First published in 1985
by Bossiney Books
St Teath, Bodmin, Cornwall
Typeset, printed and bound in Great Britain
by A. Wheaton & Co. Ltd, Exeter.

ISBN 0 948158 09 3

Front cover by Mark Bygrave

About the Author — and the Book

Jillian Powell was educated at Norwich High School and Newnham College, Cambridge, where she was awarded Double First Class Honours in English. After leaving Cambridge, she went on to study the History of Art at the Courtauld Institute, London. She now divides her time between London and the country, working as a freelance writer and teaching English and Art History.

Early in 1985, Jillian Powell made her debut for Bossiney, contributing two excellent chapters in *Westcountry Mysteries*, introduced by Colin Wilson: one on the Beast of Exmoor, the other on the disappearance of Genette Tate. She is currently working on a book of notorious paintings.

Here Jillian Powell, accompanied by photographer Julia Davey, explores *The Quantocks* in Somerset. Their sensitive combination of words and pictures — all especially commissioned for this book — produce a delightful portrait of the area.

Coleridge and the Wordsworths, history and legend, present-day exploration across these varied landscapes all combine to make this an important contribution to the Library of Somerset and country-lovers everywhere.

Introduction

A white hind in the forests, 'hunky punks' climbing the church towers and a temple-hut dedicated to Robin Hood, are just some of the hidden treasures of the Quantocks.

The Quantock villages, too, seem hidden, like Enmore or Bicknoller, glimpsed across fields and enveloped in dark summer foliage, their russet roofs and rosy church towers drinking up the colour of the Somerset soil. Villages appear suddenly before you, like Over Stowey in the dip of a hill, compact and complete in its picturesque grouping of church and cottages, or steeply-perched Aisholt, secreted in a

'The villages seem hidden, glimpsed across fields and enveloped in dark summer foliage.' Below: Enmore, Right: Bicknoller.

'Steeply-perched Aisholt, secreted in a deep, wooded valley . . .' The thatched school-house where the poet Sir Henry Newbolt lived.

deep, wooded valley, its tiny church and thatched cottages shrouded by the trees.

Tucked away, sheltered by the hills, each village is permeated by the sense of a close community, expressed in the perfect, familial grouping of church, manor house and cottages. At East Quantoxhead, where the history of the Luttrell family at Court House stretches back to the Norman Conquest, ducks on a mill-pond complete the very English picture of the Court House and church, set between the sea and the hills and built from the local grey lias stone quarried from the coast.

Yet the secret, secluded character of the Quantock villages, which has made some, like Aisholt and Nether Stowey, the favourite haunt of poets, con-

trasts dramatically with the sweeping, panoramic views afforded by the hills. The Quantocks are a walker's paradise, offering infinite variety within a compact range of hills which stretches only twelve miles from just north of Taunton to Watchet on the Bristol Channel coast. Although they rise to no more than 1260 feet at their highest point, the heathy uplands, criss-crossed by ancient trackways, provide spectacular, unbroken views across the Somerset countryside, inspiring a sense of space and drama nourished by local history and legend.

On Cothelstone Beacon, where fires were lit to warn of the threatening Spanish Armada, and on Longstone Hill, where a mysterious upright stone stands embedded almost 1000 feet above sea level, is open heathland, carpeted with springy heathers, gorse and bracken. Trees are shaped and stunted by the winds, and the grazing is rough, broken by gorse thickets, hollies and gnarled hawthorns. Buzzards circle and the meadow pipit parachutes overhead, while below lies very different country.

Here, are the rich farmlands of Taunton Deane with their patchwork of fields and dark copses clustering around stone-built farmhouses, the broad-leaved woodlands skirting Bagborough Hill, and the sheared skyline of the coniferous Quantock forest in the parish of Over Stowey. From the top of Will's Neck, at 1260 feet the highest point of the Quantocks, the countryside circles out to a dazzling 360 degree panorama, stretching west to the wooded Brendon Hills and beyond them to Exmoor, north to the silvery Bristol Channel with the Welsh coast beyond and the far Brecon Beacons, and south west to Dartmoor. Amidst all this, the Quantocks rise, an

Court House, East Quantoxhead.

6

'These woods are rich in legend.'

island or 'inlier' of old, hard rocks surrounded by the younger red sandstones, their eastern side falling away in rolling foothills, their western scarp more abrupt. Sheep and hill ponies graze on the heathy uplands, while lower down, the deep, shady combes are the haunt of the red deer, the fox, badger and adder.

It is in the woods around Bagborough that the white hind has been spotted, glimpsed almost daily against the Quantock skyline. A brilliant and rare white, mercifully respected by stag-hunt and poachers alike, she has become part of the Quantock landscape — a landscape that was once a royal forest between the Saxon estates of Cannington and Williton. Patches of the traditional Quantock woodland remain, carpeted with a soft, rich humus, canopied with the broad-leaved foliage of oak and beech, and supporting an abundance of animal and plant life. These woods, with their hollies and rowan, honeysuckle and bluebells, are rich in legend.

In the haunted wood of Shervage, the story goes, a voracious dragon, the Gurt Vurm, slept and fed on the flesh of humans, until a woodcutter,mistaking it for a log, sat down to drink, and feeling it move, struck it dead with his axe. At Walford's Gibbet, history became legend when John Walford, a local charcoal burner, was hanged in chains for the murder of his wife, her body dumped, the story has it, in Dead Woman's Ditch. These were the woods that Wordsworth and his sister Dorothy explored on long walks noted in Dorothy's *Alfoxton Journal* — woods,

The White Hind, photographed by Peter Sealy, of Bagborough.

she wrote, 'as wild as fancy ever painted'. Even their names — Kingscliff, Duke's Plantation, Parsonage Wood — breathe history.

History is all around in the Quantocks landscape, in the Bronze-Age barrows, the hill-top cairns, the earthworks, as at Trendle Ring above Bicknoller, and in the Iron-Age fort of Ruborough Camp where, local legend relates, demons guard the secret Moneyfield, an underground hoard of gold. Ancient trackways wander over the hills, like the Great Road which runs above Alfoxton Park, beneath the avenue of gnarled and twisting Holford beeches, and the old Pack Way which can be traced from Durleigh and Enmore to Cothelstone, over Bagborough Hill and down into St Audries near the Severn Estuary.

Will's Neck, where walkers pause by the Trig stone to enjoy cool breezes, birdsong and panoramic views, may have been named after a fierce battle between the Celtic 'Wealas' tribe and the invading Saxons, and near the harbour town of Watchet, raided repeatedly by the Danes, lies the field named Battlegore.

The mellow Quantock churches with their rosy, weathered towers alive with grinning gargoyles and grotesque little 'hunky punks' struggling up their sides, bear witness to quieter and more prosperous times. The thriving wool-weaving industry of the Middle Ages contributed to these fine Somerset churches with their pinnacled towers, canopied niches and delicate, pierced panelling.

Kingston St Mary is the gem of the Quantock group, its gracefully proportioned tower standing proud against the slope of the hills behind, and dominating the surrounding scenery. Here, as at Cannington and Crowcombe, Bishop's Lydeard and

'The Quantocks are a walker's paradise.'

'Kingston St Mary is the gem of "the Quantock group".'

'Will's Neck, where walkers pause by the Trig Stone to enjoy cool breezes, bird song and panoramic views.'

Bicknoller, the local red sandstone has mellowed to a dusky pink silvered by lichen. The decoration is exuberant, from the pierced battlements and tiers of lacy, quatrefoil tracery to the mischievous hunky punks clambering up the corners of the tower. This playful exuberance is repeated in the richly-carved Tudor bench-ends within — one showing a weaver's shuttle identical to that used by the neighbouring Church Farm Weavers today.

The oak bench ends in the Quantock churches are a treasury of Quantock legend, lore, trades and crafts. At Spaxton a fuller appears with his tools, at Kingston a team of oxen and yokes, at Bishop's Lydeard we see a Quantock stag and a windmill dodged by the birds, at Stogursey a rare spoonbill

13

14

and at Crowcombe, two men tussling, St George-like, with a dragon. Everywhere flowers, vines and rosaries sprout and twist with an almost pagan vitality. In some, the imagery has been lost to us, others — like the weaver's shuttle at Kingston — bear witness to the continuing crafts and traditions of the Quantocks.

In a converted, thirteenth-century cider barn next door to the church of Kingston St Mary, the Church Farm Weavers, John Lennon and Talbot Potter, carry on traditions of hand dyeing, spinning and weaving, which stretch back centuries. Their work reflects, and is nourished by, the Quantock countryside, as they use local fleeces hand dyed with subtle plant hues such as walnut, madder, heather and privet. They hand spin and weave the wool into rugs, tweeds, wall-hangings and ecclesiastical ware for churches all over the country and abroad — including neighbouring St Mary's. Its own mellow, silvered tower has provided the inspiration for the colouring of eighty yards of cloth woven for the 'Quaker tapestry', to be embroidered by some seventy Meeting Houses in time, it is hoped, for the 1989 Edinburgh Festival.

Here, in their hand-loom weaving workshop, the Church Farm Weavers practise and teach their craft, as the Quantock Weavers, Miss Biddulph and Miss Dickinson, did for forty years before them at the Old Forge, Plainsfield. The Quantock Weavers became known throughout Somerset for their intricate hand-weaving, inspired by the patterns of rock strata and dyed using plants from the hills — gorse, lichens, sloe and whortleberry. Now, the Old Forge has become a

'The Church bench-ends are a treasury of Quantock legend, lore, trades and crafts.' Far left: Spaxton, the fuller and his tools. Left: Kingston, oxen and yokes.

Window of the Old Forge, in the hamlet of Plainsfield near Over Stowey.

weaving workshop once again, with Wendy Cobbledick and Venetia Taylor using local Jacob and Border Leicester fleeces, hand knitted or woven into clothing, rugs, wall hangings and furnishings.

The give-and-take relationship between the Quantock craftsman and his environment is demonstrated again at Stogumber, where Ralph Farrer makes handmade furniture using hardwoods including local beech, ash, burr elm and burr oak, and at Williton where potter Martin Pettinger, using local clays and traditional Somerset styles and techniques, creates hand-thrown pots vibrant with motifs of the Quantock countryside. Kingfishers, badgers, butterflies,

15

stags, heather and dragonflies adorn pots, vases and plates decorated with a variety of traditional slip techniques dating back to the fourteenth century and ranging from marbling, carving and trailing to eighteenth century Mocha.

Here, traditional techniques, colours and styles — the essence of the Somerset tradition — are being kept alive, and invigorated, with new ideas, combinations and designs. When we visited his Williton workshop, Martin Pettinger was working on a range of 'Audubon' pots destined for America, fine pots decorated with the brilliant and beautiful designs of Audubon's bird drawings, using the traditional *sgraffiato* or carving technique. His aim is to make such fine, hand techniques practical and affordable, creating a marriage between the past and the present which reflects a characteristic quality of the Quantock landscape itself.

In countryside rich in the associations of history and poetry, many places have taken on new and sometimes unexpected rôles in the life of the Quantocks today. At Hestercombe, where Edwin Lutyens and Gertrude Jekyll created a masterpiece of garden design, the peaceful gardens with their graceful, balustraded walks, shady arbours and cool lily ponds contrasts dramatically with the billowing smoke and authoritative shouts of trainee firemen staging a practice rescue beind the walls of Lutyens' elegant orangery. Hestercombe House, once the home of the Portman family, is now the headquarters of the Somerset Fire Brigade, under whose auspices the gardens are being so beautifully restored.

Over at Halsway Manor, the imposing battlemented house where Cardinal Beaufort is reputed to have stayed, the rhythmic beat of the tambourine floats out over sweeping lawns — for here is the Centre for English folk song and dance run

16

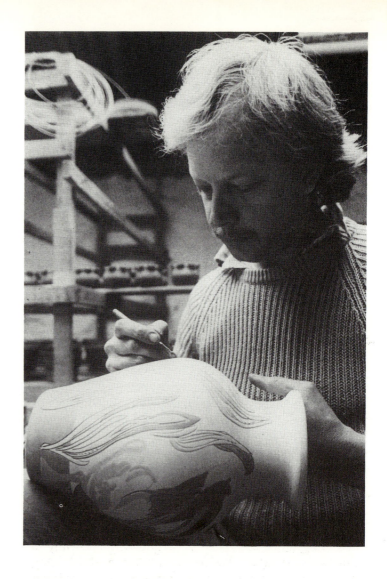

Williton potter, Martin Pettinger.

'At Hestercombe, the peaceful gardens contrast dramatically with the billowing smoke and authoritative shouts of trainee firemen staging a practice rescue.'

by the Halsway Manor Society. Halsway's history stretches back to a site mentioned in the Domesday Book, further even than that of the Benedictine Priory at Cannington, founded in the twelfth century and now the site of the Somerset College of Agriculture and Horticulture. Nearby Brymore, once the home of the great Parliamentarian John Pym, is now a Technical Agricultural School, while Fyne Court at Broomfield, where Andrew Crosse performed his pioneer experiments in electricity, is leased by the National Trust to the Somerset Trust for Nature Conservation.

The National Trust now owns the little cottage in Nether Stowey where a clear brook once flowed by the front door, and Coleridge wrote *Christabel*, *The Ancient Mariner* and *Frost at Midnight*. From here, Coleridge would walk to see the Wordsworths at Alfoxton Park, the white, ivy-clad Queen Anne House, now an hotel, set in a hollow on the slopes of the Quantock hills. The poets' inspiration is all around in the countryside, in the pink and grey, windswept shores of Kilve, where smugglers lugged kegs of brandy to the ruined chantry, as in the busy, blowy harbour town of Watchet, whence Coleridge's Ancient Mariner set sail on his fateful voyage.

The Quantocks are resonant with echoes of the past, sometimes sinister, as at Cothelstone gatehouse where two of Monmouth's men were hanged, sometimes poignant, as at West Bagborough, where a mysterious, cloaked statue of a man and his dog surveys the view from a prospect seat — an isolated symbol of the eighteenth century park of vanished Tirhill House.

'The busy, blowy harbour town of Watchet, whence
Coleridge's Ancient Mariner set sail.'

'Bullocks wander in and out between the columns, where once tea parties were held' — the Ionic Temple folly at Halswell House.

More unexpected still, is the graceful little Ionic temple which appears in a farmer's field by the Goathurst road, capped with ivy and sprouting with ash and sycamore. Bullocks wander in and out between the columns, over leaves and rubble where once tea parties were held — for this is one of the follies of nearby Halswell House, whose wooded park, it was said, bore the 'stamp of pleasure'. Halswell's imposing façade can be seen from the temple and, tucked up against the woods behind it, is the little hut dedicated to Robin Hood, where evening barbecues were held after a hunt in the woods beyond.

The hidden follies of Halswell are poignant reminders of a lost age, in a landscape which, in spite of its timeless appearance, is constantly changing and evolving. Much of the traditional broadleaved woodland has given way to the high-yielding soft wood conifers of the Forestry Commission. Farming, grazing, touring, riding, even walking affect — and can injure — the countryside. Seen from Taunton or the Mendips, the Quantocks look timeless with their sinuous, gently rolling skyline. Yet, like a microcosm of the English countryside, they exist in delicate balance — and need protection.

One of the first landmarks the traveller by rail sees as he approaches Taunton is the arched silhouette of the Seven Sisters, the wind-shaped beeches on the top of Cothelstone Beacon. The trees are old, but, nearby, a group of young beeches has been planted — a hopeful symbol in the living, changing Quantock landscape.

19

History in the Landscape

The grassy ramparts which mark the site of
the Norman Castle at Nether Stowey. Traces
of the keep foundations remain on the
'mount', which was used in the nineteenth
century for bear-baiting and rough sports.

The Longstone, a mysterious upright stone embedded 952 feet above sea level on Longstone Hill, near the path leading westwards to the Great Road and Bicknoller Post.

Castle Ruins

Medieval Castle ruins at Stogursey — and a
fairytale conversion complete with
drawbridge (left) and moat (above).

Places of Birth . . .

Brymore, Cannington, now a Technical
Agricultural School, was the home of the great
seventeenth-century Parliamentarian, John
Pym. The porch survives from the house that
Pym knew.

Townsend House, East Quantoxhead was in 1784 the birthplace of Sarah Biffen, the armless painter who, after sixteen years travelling as a side-act with city fairs and circus shows, was befriended by the Earl of Morton. Sarah became renowned for her delicate portrait miniatures, painted using her mouth, and enjoyed the patronage of royalty.

. . . And Places of Death

Walford's Gibbet (above) marks the site where, in the eighteenth century, John Walford, a local charcoal burner, was hanged after murdering his wife in a drunken rage. Here, among the gnarled oaks and stunted hollies, his body hung in chains for a full twelve months before it was removed. Local legend relates that nearby Dead Woman's Ditch (right) is the place where Walford dumped his wife's body, but the sinister name preceded Walford's crime, and was probably coined after the remains of a traveller were found on this prehistoric land boundary.

The outer gate posts at Cothelstone Manor,
where two of Monmouth's men were hanged
by Judge Jeffreys for their part in the Pitch-
fork Rebellion of 1685.

The Battle of Sedgemoor, The Pitchfork Rebellion

Quantock men were among the rebels who
took up pitchforks and scythes, and fought for
the Duke of Monmouth at the Battle of
Sedgemoor on 6 July 1685. Here, at the Sealed
Knot reconstruction for the 300th anniversary
of the Battle — the last to be fought on English
soil — the opposing troops advance and (left)
women and children watch their menfolk on
the battlefield.

Hills

Left: The Seven Sisters, Cothelstone Beacon.
Above: Walkers on Will's Neck, at 1260 feet
the highest point on the Quantocks. The Trig
stone, one of the Beacons of the South West,
offers a dazzling 360-degree panorama of the
Somerset countryside.

Woods

Above: Trees against the skyline, Kingscliff
Wood.

Left: Forestry Commission land,
Cockercombe.

Right: Forestry Commission workers
measuring and cutting lengths of softwood
for pulp and fencing.

Sea Shore

The ivy-clad ruins of the fifteenth-century chantry in Kilve Lane, where smugglers hid kegs of brandy among bales of hay. The chantry was burned down in 1848, perhaps to foil the investigations of excise officers, who might have found casks in such unlikely places as the church tower!

Right: The pink and grey, windswept shores of Kilve, with their jagged terraces of shale and lias rich in ammonites, or 'St Keyna's serpents', according to the tradition that the Saint turned all the snakes on the shore to stone. Here, Wordsworth walked along 'Kilve's smooth shore by the green sea', with his sister Dorothy, and at the time of the Napoleonic Wars, the lonely creek was used by smugglers, who transported their booty in farm wagons loaded with straw or turnips.

Wildlife

Sheep, after shearing, near Dead Woman's
Ditch.

Right: Quantock hill ponies, and foal.

Durleigh Reservoir

Durleigh reservoir, haven for birds and popular with local still-water anglers fishing for brown and rainbow trout. Over 160 species of bird have been recorded in the sanctuary at Durleigh, including grebes, herons, cormorants, ospreys and, in winter, some 200 Bewick's swans from Siberia. Across the water is the turreted manor house said to be the birthplace of Jane Seymour. At low water, the manor's carp ponds can be seen, along with cottage foundations and the tree stumps of orchards now covered by the lowland reservoir.

Triumphant Bridgwater angler Reg Mansell with his prize catch — a rainbow trout which weighed in at over 6 lb, big enough to qualify for the monthly Trout Masters' Competition. Reg has been fishing since he was eight years old.

40

Left: Three times a day, reservoir ranger Bob Jones feeds the trout in the rearing tanks with a high-protein pellet of fish and cereal. In this tank, there are some 1200 fish from the Clatworthy hatcheries, which will be graded regularly (right) and moved into the 80-acre reservoir when they are 12 inches or more in length.

Quantock Crafts

In a converted thirteenth-century Cider Barn next door to the Church of Kingston St Mary, the Church Farm Weavers, John Lennon and Talbot Potter, make tweeds, furnishing fabrics, rugs, wall hangings and ecclesiastical ware, using local fleeces which are hand-dyed with plant dyes, before being hand-spun and woven in their workshop. They aim to keep alive the traditions of the Somerset Wool

Weaving Industry and to encourage imaginative design in industry, as well as creating fabrics which are unique in colour and pattern.

At the Old Forge, Over Stowey, where the Quantock Weavers, Miss Biddulph and Miss Dickinson, worked for forty years, Wendy Cobbledick and Venetia Taylor run a workshop where Wendy knits and weaves the natural coloured, hand-spun fleeces of her own Jacob and Border Leicester sheep, and Venetia makes garments, furnishings and 'rolag' work, for which she uses machine-carded, unspun wool. Here, Venetia is working at the loom, weaving rolag in a traditional rose-path pattern.

At the Williton Pottery (right), Martin Pettinger continues the Somerset tradition of making decorative slipware pottery from Westcountry clays, re-creating many of the old styles of Somerset pottery dating back to the fourteenth century. The colours are rich and resonant, ranging from warm honey glazes to deep cobalt blues; the motifs are culled from the Quantock countryside and include kingfishers, badgers, stags, decorative heathers and dancing dragonflies. Vases, jugs, lamp bases, plates and bowls are all hand-thrown on the wheel and decorated with traditional hand-techniques including marbling, trailing and carving. Here (left), Martin Pettinger is using the *sgraffito* or carving technique to decorate a vase inspired by Audubon's drawing of mallards. The 'Audubon range' — destined for the gift fairs of America — combines traditional techniques with brilliance of design, and introduces the idea of the 'picture pot' — for every pot tells a story.

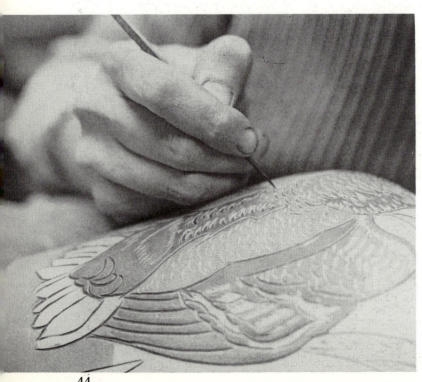

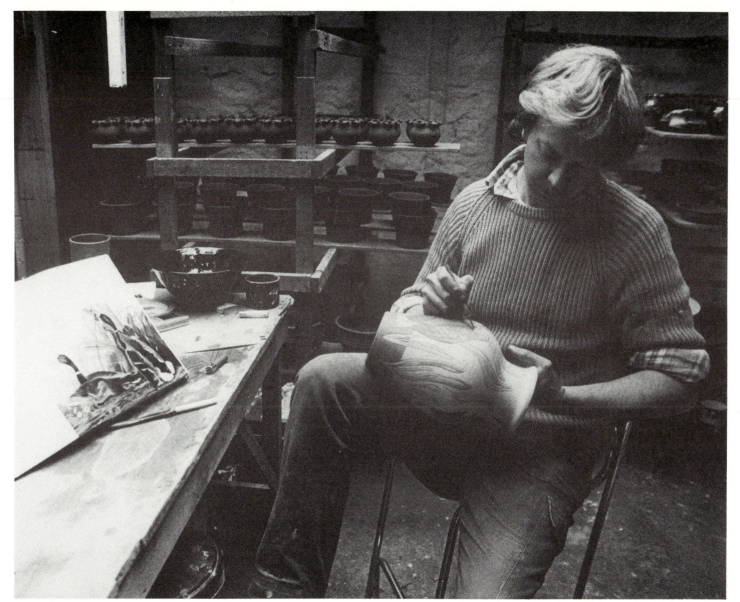

Ralph Farrer in his Stogumber showroom. In
the workshops below, he makes hand-made
furniture from tables and chairs to solitaire
boards and glass mats in quality hardwoods
such as beech, walnut, ash, burr oak and the
warm, Brazilian mahogany.

46

The Way. Book cover showing intricate drawn, pulled and cut work by embroidery specialist Oenone Cave, who exhibits batik-dyed silks, miniature hand-weavings, traditional smocking and Greek lace or 'Ruskin work' at her Rambler studio in Holford. Here, her daughter Sylvia specialises in botanical plant drawings and glass engraving — both inspired by the flowers and wildlife of the Quantocks.

48

Quantock Thatch

Left: The thatched dovecote which belonged
to the monks of the twelfth-century Priory at
Stogursey.
Above: Thatched cottages at Crowcombe.

Quantock Churches

Crowcombe Church of the Holy Ghost
contains one of the finest collections of Tudor
bench ends in Somerset.

North Petherton Church, with its 120-feet highly-decorated Perpendicular tower. The Alfred Jewel was found in this parish — once the seat of Ina, King of the West Saxons. Outside the graveyard, excavations uncovered Christian Saxon burials, including one of a 7-foot giant, with a dagger in his hand.

Church Treasures

The fine, fan-vaulted rood screen in the Church of St Mary the Virgin, Bishop's Lydeard, decorated with leaden stars and intricate tracery carvings and inscribed with the Apostles' Creed in Latin. The screen, of the West-of-England type, is believed to have been made in Taunton in the early sixteenth-century.

Above: The Vernay tomb in the Norman Church of St Andrew, Stogursey. In 1442, John de Vernay had to appear before the Archbishop of Canterbury — for shouting at the vicar in English during a Latin Mass.

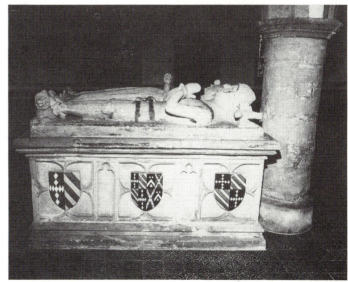

Right: The fourteenth-century stone effigies of Sir Matthew de Stawell and his wife Eleonor Merton, in the Stawell Chapel of Cothelstone Church. His feet rest on lions, hers on two playful squirrels.

Quantock Gargoyles

Quantock gargoyles at (above) Cannington, Church of St Mary the Virgin and (right and far right) at Stogumber, Church of St Mary.

Quantock Villages — Crowcombe

The mellow eighteenth-century brick and
Ham-stone façade of Crowcombe Court,
home of the Carews, where once peacocks
strutted over the lawns.

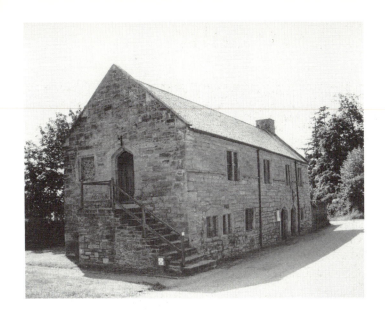

A rare, surviving Medieval Church House, where Church Ales and village festivities were held. An adjoining animal pound was fenced off for stray animals awaiting collection by their owners.

The weathered Market Cross, dating from the days when Crowcombe was a borough, and intended to remind villagers to be just Christians in buying and selling — and to be good neighbours.

Stogumber

Left: Tired of waiting for her betrothed, Sir Francis Drake, to return from sea, Lady Elisabeth Sydenham set out for her wedding to a rival suitor in Stogumber Church. But as she walked to the church, a fiery meteorite shot across her path, landing at her feet. 'Drake's cannon had fired a volley across the world' — and Lady Sydenham returned, unwed, to wait for Drake's return. The legendary cannon-ball is kept in the Hall at Combe Sydenham, where it is reputed to bring good fortune to all who touch it.

The Seven Crosses. One of the Medieval doorways with decorative ironwork and hinges which adorn the Seven Crosses in Stogumber, a conversion from two cottages which used to be church property.

Bicknoller

The village of Bicknoller enchanted nineteenth-century Nature writer Richard Jefferies, who described it in *Summer in Somerset*. The Perpendicular church has its original Medieval stone altar.

Under the umbrella of an ancient yew are the old village stocks. One of the 1932 bench ends in the church shows another yew which, sown by a bird, sprouted from the top of the fifteenth-century sandstone tower.

Enmore

Left: One of the rounded corner towers survives at Enmore Castle, built in the eighteenth century by John Perceval, Earl of Egmont who, according to Dr Johnson, was addicted to 'romantic projects and airy speculations'. The castellated, sandstone castle was built with a turreted gate-house, a drawbridge over a 40-foot dry moat, and underground offices and stables — a fitting residence for the Earl, who tried by Act of Parliament to restore the old feudal system in England.

Right: The sign of the Tynte Arms, Enmore, showing the armorial bearings of the Tynte family of Halswell House — a white lion and six white crosses on a blood-red shield. The bearings are said to have been conferred by Richard Lionheart on a young knight of the house of Arundel, after his clothes had been stained (tinted) red with the blood of Saracens at the battle of Ascalon. The present Inn was converted from two cottages, given in the nineteenth century by the Tynte family to a favoured butler.

63

Enmore

The School house at Enmore, one of the first free primary schools in England, built in 1810 and paid for by the rent from six cottages built by the Reverend John Poole, rector of Enmore for 60 years. The village has been called 'the cradle of free elementary education in this country'.

West Bagborough

Village cricket, Bagborough versus Over Stowey. Villagers were leaning over a roadside gate to watch this match played out in evening sunlight.

Halswell House, Goathurst

The imposing façade of Halswell House, begun in 1689 by Sir Halswell Tynte, and once graced with Grinling Gibbons carvings, fine plasterwork ceilings and paintings by Lely and Van Dyck. The 230-acre park, renowned for its majestic trees and a thriving heronry, was studded with follies, including a stepped pyramid 'in honour of a pure maiden', a memorial to a horse, a temple dedicated to Robin Hood, a grotto, and a classical rotunda. Arthur Young wrote of the park in the eighteenth century 'the whole scene is really elegant, every part is *riant* and bears the stamp of pleasure'.

Above: The pyramid 'in honour of a pure maiden'.
Right: The rotunda, now the haunt of bats, overgrown with trees and cascading ivy. Beneath is an underground ice-house.

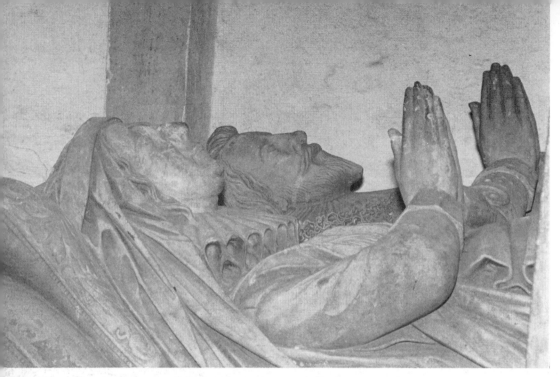

The effigies of Sir Nicholas Halswell and his wife Bridgett in the Halswell Aisle of Goathurst Church. Bridgett, who died in 1627, requested burial in the chapel, adding: 'What would I not give that the bones of my faithfull and dear Nicke were brought over and buried with me.' Here, they lie together, their heads on tasselled cushions, their sarcophagus guarded by the weeping figures of their nine children.

Tucked up against the woods at Halswell is the little hut dedicated to Robin Hood, where evening barbecues were held after a hunt in the woods beyond.

Quantock Villages — Nether Stowey

Rider and horses returning along Castle Street
to the stables in Nether Stowey. On this street
is the house where the self-taught man of
culture and friend of Coleridge's, Tom Poole,
had his tannery and his book room. A
pathway led through the lime trees in his
garden to Coleridge's cottage in Lime Street
(opposite).

Coleridge's Cottage in Lime Street, Nether Stowey, where the poet lived from 1796–9 and wrote *The Ancient Mariner*, *Christabel* and *Frost at Midnight*. In the stone-floored parlour is his brass-inlaid Boulle ink-stand, his sword, and three locks of his hair. Wordsworth and his sister Dorothy walked here from Alfoxton Park.

Shoeing a horse at the farriery, Nether
Stowey.

David Toogood (right) has been shoeing Quantock horses for some 25 years in his workshops at Nether Stowey and St Audries. The beams around the workshop are studded with old shoes — one believed to be the shoe of a working bullock.

The gnarled and windswept Holford beeches,
along the Great Road on Longstone Hill.

The white, Queen Anne House, now an hotel,
where the Wordsworths lived from 1797–8
until they came under suspicion of being
French spies. Here, they were visited by
Charles Lamb, Thomas de Quincey, Robert
Southey and Josiah Wedgwood — and out of
their close companionship with Coleridge at
Nether Stowey, sprang the Lyrical Ballads. In
the grounds is the oak noted by Dorothy in
her Alfoxton Journal, in which she describes
the hills, deep combes and distant views to
Steep Holm and Flat Holm, observed on long
walks through the Quantocks by day and after
dark. 'There is everything here,' she wrote,
'sea and woods wild as fancy ever painted.'

Watchet

The busy, blowy harbour of Watchet,
resonant with sea shanties, whence
Coleridge's Ancient Mariner set sail on his
fateful voyage:

The ship was cheered, the harbour cleared
Merrily did we drop
Below the kirk, below the hill,
Below the light-house top.

Right: Coastal view from Watchet harbour, an
important Victorian coasting port for timber,
Welsh coal and iron ore from the Brendon
Hills, Watchet harbour now serves the paper
mills behind the town.

The thirteenth-century church of St Decumen, Watchet. Inside, a wall brass commemorates Florence Wyndham, who is said to have come back from the dead. Her coffin was lying in the church when the sexton, unable to resist the thought of her fine rings, prised it open. To his horror, Florence awoke as if from a trance and rose up, shrouded. She returned to her home at Kentisford, where she lived happily for many years, and gave birth to the son who commemorated her here.

St Decumen's Well. The sixth-century monk
St Decumen, legend has it, journeyed from
Wales on a raft, with only a faithful cow for
company and sustenance. In Watchet he
lived as a hermit until a hostile Dane struck off
his head as he prayed. Still, his body rose up,
carefully washed his head in this well, and
replaced it on his shoulders — so the story
goes.

Ghosts

At Halsway Manor the 'White Lady' wanders in search of her husband, as she has done since his grave was moved after her own death.

The Plough at Holford — where Virginia and
Leonard Woolf honeymooned — is said to be
haunted by the ghost of a Spanish merchant,
murdered for his hoard of gold.

Devil Legends

Ruborough Camp, Broomfield Hill. The Iron Age Fort of Ruborough, beneath which lies the legendary Moneyfield, a castle full of gold, entered by an iron door and guarded by demons. In the eighteenth century, one Dr Farrer and his manservant went digging for treasure by the light of the full moon, and, so the story goes, narrowly escaped being dragged underground by shrieking demons.

Right: The Old Forge, Fiddington, a fairytale cottage where one stormy night a mysterious dark rider stopped to have his horse shod, and sent the smith running to the village priest — for the traveller was none other than the Devil himself.

Quantock Legend

The haunted wood of Shervage where, legend has it, the Gurt Vurm, a serpent-like dragon as thick as three oak trees, slept and fed on the flesh of humans. Cattle and sheep, too, were devoured whole, and ponies disappeared, until a woodcutter picking whortleberries in the woods, sat down to drink, and, feeling the log beneath him begin to move, struck it with his axe, cutting the Vurm in two.

— and History

Left: Cannington Priory, now the Somerset College of Agriculture and Horticulture. Fragments of the wall survive from the Priory of Benedictine nuns founded in the twelfth century, where, according to legend, Fair Rosamond de Clifford was brought up.

Right: Fyne Court, Broomfield, leased by the National Trust to the Somerset Trust for Nature Conservation. Here, was the home of Andrew Crosse, the wealthy Quantock squire known as 'the thunder and lightning man' on account of his pioneer experiments with electricity which, some say, inspired Mary Shelley to write the Frankenstein story.

Legend — and History

The Chapel of the 'Abode of Love' at Spaxton. Here, the Reverend Henry John Prince founded the notorious Agapemonite Sect, which was said to have turned 'the beautiful little hamlet into a wilderness of particularly repulsive vices'. 'Brother Prince', and later his successor the Reverend John Hugh Smyth-Pigott, initiated wealthy and attractive women into the sect by ritual and sexual union with 'The Heavenly Bridegroom'. A rich and gullible coterie followed Prince, and later Smyth-Pigott as the New Messiah, pooling their incomes to become a 'soul bride' or 'spiritual wife' of their leader. Both men were un-frocked by the church for their immoral conduct, and in 1927, Smyth-Pigott's death prompted a furore of reaction in the Press.

A chapel window in the 'Abode of Love' at Spaxton.

The Gardens at Hestercombe House, near Kingston St Mary

Gertrude Jekyll worked with Edwin Lutyens
at Hestercombe between 1904–9 and many
believe these graceful gardens, with their
measured walkways, shady arbours, cool rills
and inviting, stone-arched doorways, to be
their finest work together. The sunken plat
(left) offers a myriad of patterned vistas,
framed by an oak-beamed pergola and
playful, stone-ribboned rills carrying rivulets
of water to knots of irises, forget-me-nots
and arum lilies. Behind Lutyens' classical,
garlanded orangery (above) trainee firemen
tackle a blazing oil barrel, for Hestercombe is
now the headquarters of the Somerset Fire
Brigade.

89

Patterns at Hestercombe

The interplay of art and Nature — in shadow, reflections, colour, texture and form. The pergola (left) which runs along the southern boundary of the formal garden, carries trailing pink roses, vines and forsythia, and offers views across the old tennis court and orchard to the Vale of Taunton and the Blackdown Hills. At either end, keyhole windows pierce the walls and wisterias frame the gateways leading East and West out of the garden. Hostas and ornamental thistles are among the drifts of plants which spill from the borders, and circular lily ponds (right) feed the rills which run the length of the garden.

From Formal Gardens to Open Spaces

ALSO AVAILABLE

UNKNOWN BRISTOL
by Rosemary Clinch. 75 illustrations.
An unusual exploration of this romantic city. The author has stopped to talk to people and asked the kind of questions that intrigue all of us.
'Not a normal guide . . . it's a lovely book and very interesting . . .'
Penny Downs, Radio Bristol

WESTCOUNTRY MYSTERIES
Introduced by Colin Wilson. 45 illustrations.
A team of authors probe mysterious happenings in Somerset, Devon and Cornwall. Drawings and photographs all add to the mysterious content.
'. . . unresolved stories from past and present. Most beguiling is David Foot's essay on Thomas Shoel, the 18th century composer from Somerset. I would buy the book for that story alone . . .'
Margaret Smith, Express and Echo

STRANGE SOMERSET STORIES
Introduced by David Foot with chapters by Ray Waddon, Jack Hurley, Lornie Leete-Hodge, Hilary Wreford, David Foot, Rosemary Clinch and Michael Williams.
'. . . a good collection of yarns about Somerset's eccentrics, weird legends and architectural follies . . .'
Dan Lees, The Western Daily Press

SOMERSET IN THE OLD DAYS
by David Young. 145 old photographs.
David Young of TSW takes a journey in words and old pictures across Somerset.
'Illustrated by a charm-filled collection of old photographs, David Young's book fairly reeks of nostalgia.'
The Western Morning News

EXMOOR IN THE OLD DAYS
by Rosemary Anne Lauder. 147 photographs.
The author perceptively shows that Exmoor is not only the most beautiful of our Westcountry moors but is also rich in history and character: a world of its own in fact.
'. . . contains scores of old photographs and picture postcards . . . will provide a passport for many trips down memory lane . . .'
Bideford Gazette

CURIOSITIES OF SOMERSET
By Lornie Leete-Hodge. 73 illustrations.
A look at some of the unusual and sometimes strange aspects of Somerset – completing a Curiosities hat-trick for Bossiney.
'Words and pictures combine to capture that unique quality that is Somerset.'
Western Gazette

GHOSTS OF SOMERSET
by Peter Underwood. 48 illustrations.
As President of the Ghost Club, the author has probably heard more ghost stories than any man alive. A look at a variety of ghostly encounters.
'. . . ghostly encounters that together make up the rich tapestry of the Ghosts of Somerset.'
Western Gazette

LEGENDS OF SOMERSET
by Sally Jones. 65 photographs and drawings.
Sally Jones travels across rich legendary landscapes. Words, drawings and photographs all combine to evoke a spirit of adventure.
'On the misty lands of the Somerset Plain – as Sally Jones makes clear – history, legend and fantasy are inextricably mixed.'
Dan Lees, The Western Daily Press

DARTMOOR IN THE OLD DAYS
by James Mildren. 145 photographs.
James Mildren is an author who is at home in the wilderness of his Dartmoor.
'Lovers of Dartmoor will need no persuasion to obtain a copy. To anybody else, I suggest they give it a try. It may lead to a better understanding of why many people want Dartmoor to remain a wonderful wilderness.'
Keith Whitford, The Western

100 YEARS ON BODMIN MOOR
by E. V. Thompson
A rich harvest of old photographs and picture postcards, reflecting life on the Moor for a century with a perceptive text.
'. . . will entice the present day visitor to Cornwall to explore the Moor . . .'

Pamela Luke, The Methodist Recorder

DISCOVERING BODMIN MOOR

By E. V. Thompson. 45 photographs and map.
E. V. Thompson, author of the bestselling novel, *Chase the Wind*, set on the eastern slopes of Bodmin Moor, explores the Moor past and present.
'. . . shows the moor in all its aspects – beautiful, harsh, romantic and almost cruel . . . how well he knows the character of the moor.'
The Editor, Cornish Guardian

SUPERSTITION AND FOLKLORE

by Michael Williams. 45 photographs.
Romany reflections, old country customs, interviews with superstitious people, folklore from both Devon and Cornwall, omens and coincidences are all featured.
'. . . has all the ingredients of a mini-bestseller.'
Cornwall Courier

SEA STORIES OF CORNWALL

by Ken Duxbury. 48 photographs.
'This is a tapestry of true tales', writes the author, 'by no means all of them disasters – which portray something of the spirit, the humour, the tragedy, and the enchantment, that is the lot of we who know the sea.'
'Ken is a sailor, and these stories are written with a close understanding and feel for the incidents.'
James Mildren, The Western Morning News

RIVERS OF CORNWALL

by Sarah Foot. 130 photographs, 45 in colour.
The author explores six great Cornish rivers: the Helford, the Fal, the Fowey, the Camel, the Lynher and the Tamar.
' . . . makes use of many colour illustrations as well as black and white and shows that whatever changes may have taken place in the river economics they remain places of quality and beauty, quintessentially Cornwall.'
The Cornish Guardian

SEA STORIES OF DEVON

In this companion volume to *Sea Stories of Cornwall* nine Westcountry authors recall stirring events and people from Devon's sea past. Well illustrated with old and new photographs, it is introduced by best-selling novelist E. V. Thompson.
'The tales themselves are interesting and varied but the real strength of the book lies in the wealth of illustration, with photographs and pictures on practically every page.'
Jane Leigh, Express & Echo

UNKNOWN DEVON

by Rosemary Anne Lauder, Monica Wyatt and Michael Williams. 73 illustrations.
In Unknown Devon three writers explore off-the-beaten track places in Devon.
'If you want to extend your knowledge of hidden Devon then this well-illustrated book is a handy companion.'
Mid-Devon Advertiser

THE CORNISH COUNTRYSIDE

by Sarah Foot. 130 illustrations, 40 in colour.
Here, in Bossiney's first colour publication, Sarah Foot explores inland Cornwall, the moors and the valleys, and meets those who work on the land.
'Sarah Foot sets out to share her obvious passion for Cornwall and to describe its enigmas . . . It is a book for those who are already in love with Cornwall and for those who would like to know her better.'
Alison Foster, The Cornish Times

PEOPLE & PLACES IN CORNWALL

by Michael Williams. 54 photographs.
'. . . outlines ten notable characters . . . whose lives and work have been influenced by "Cornwall's genius to fire creativity" . . . a fascinating study.'
The Cornish Guardian

100 YEARS AROUND THE LIZARD

by Jean Stubbs. 150 old photographs.
'. . . the true flavour of life on the windswept peninsula, past and present . . . The strange qualities of the flat landscape, the effects of the elements on people's daily lives and, above all, the contrasts of past and present are distilled in the text.'
Cornish Life

125 YEARS WITH THE WESTERN MORNING NEWS

by James Mildren. 140 illustrations.
Looks at stories and photographs that have made the headlines in the Westcountry since its birth in 1860.
'. . . packed with wonderfully nostalgic and dramatic pictures.'
Judy Diss, Herald Express

MOUNT'S BAY

by Douglas Williams
More than 120 old photographs of an area stretching from Land's End to the Lizard with perceptive text by one of Cornwall's most respected journalists.

'. . . a fascinating and exhaustive study . . . It is a guidebook, potted history, pictorial gallery of Cornish life – all these things and very much more.'

The Western Evening Herald

AROUND LAND'S END
Michael Williams explores the end and the beginning of Cornwall. Wrecks and legends, the Minack Theatre, Cable & Wireless, Penwith characters and customs, lighthouses and Lyonesse all feature. 90 photographs, many of them from Edwardian and Victorian times, help to tell the story.
. . . a delightful stroll not only along the lanes but the legends of this celebrated area.'

The Cornishman

UNKNOWN CORNWALL
by Michael Williams
84 drawings and photographs nearly all especially commissioned for this publication, portraying features of Cornwall rarely seen on the published page.
'. . . a treasure chest of rich jewels that will surprise many people who pride themselves on a thorough knowledge . . .'

Western Evening Herald

GATEWAY TO CORNWALL
by Joan Rendell, 72 photographs.
Joan Rendell writes about Launceston and District – a highly personal portrait of the place, some of its past and people. 'I have attempted to make this book different from other publications about the area . . .'
'A delight to lovers of the local scene and its historic background.'

Arthur Venning, The Editor, Cornish & Devon Post

LEGENDS OF CORNWALL
by Sally Jones. 60 photographs and drawings.
Brilliantly illustrated with photographs and vivid drawings of legendary characters. A journey through the legendary sites of Cornwall, beginning at the Tamar and ending at Land's End.
'Highly readable and beautifully romantic . . .'

Desmond Lyons, Cornwall Courier

OCCULT IN THE WEST
by Michael Williams. Over 30 photographs.
Michael Williams follows his successful Supernatural in Cornwall with further interviews and investigations into the Occult – this time incorporating Devon. Ghosts and clairvoyancy, dreams and

psychic painting, healing and hypnosis are only some of the facets of a fascinating story.
'. . . provides the doubters with much food for thought.'

Jean Kenzie, Tavistock Gazette

STRANGE HAPPENINGS IN CORNWALL
by Michael Williams. 35 photographs.
Strange shapes, and strange characters; healing and life after death; reincarnation and Spiritualism; murders and mysteries are only some of the contents in this fascinating book.
'. . . this eerie Cornish collection.'

David Foot, Western Daily Press

CORNISH MYSTERIES
by Michael Williams. 40 photographs.
Cornish Mysteries is a kind of jigsaw puzzle in words and pictures. The power of charming, mysterious shapes in the Cornish landscape, the baffling murder case of Mrs Hearn are just some fascinating ingredients.
'. . . superstitions, dreams, murder, Lyonesse, the legendary visit of the boy Jesus to Cornwall, and much else. Splendid, and sometimes eerie, chapters.'

The Methodist Recorder

THE CRUEL CORNISH SEA
by David Mudd. 65 photographs.
David Mudd selects more than 30 Cornish shipwrecks, spanning 400 years, in his fascinating account of seas at a coastline that each year claims its toll of human lives.
'This is an important book.'

Lord St Levan, the Cornish Times

NORTH CORNWALL IN THE OLD DAYS
by Joan Rendell, 147 old photographs.
These pictures and Joan Rendell's perceptive text combine to give us many facets of a nostalgic way of North Cornish life, stretching from Newquay to the Cornwall/Devon border.
'This remarkable collection of pictures is a testimony to a people, a brave and uncomplaining race.'
Pamela Leeds, The Western Evening Herald.

We shall be pleased to send you our catalogue giving full details of our growing list of titles for Devon, Cornwall and Somerset and forthcoming publications.

If you have difficulty in obtaining our titles, write direct to Bossiney Books, Land's End, St Teath, Bodmin, Cornwall.